IN . ON . OR ABOUT THE PREMISES

"All men by nature desire to know. An indication of this is the delight we take in our senses; for even apart from their usefulness they are loved for themselves; and above all others the sense of sight. For not only with a view to action, but even when we are not going to do anything, we prefer seeing (one might say) to everything else. The reason is that this, most of all the senses, makes us know and brings to light many differences between things."

Aristotle, *Metaphysics,* I, 1.

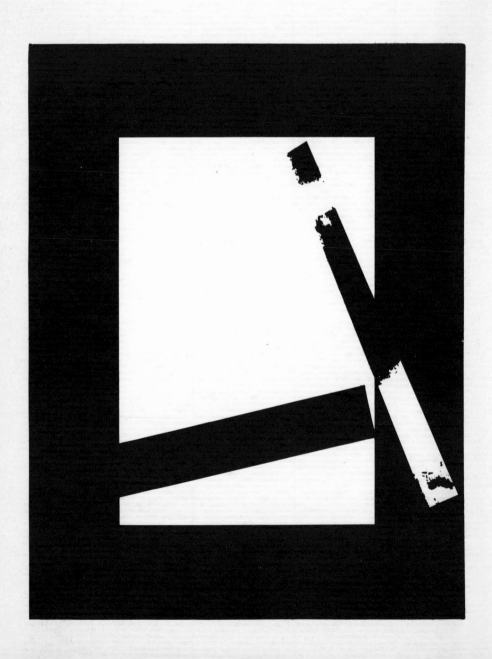

IN . ON . OR ABOUT

THE PREMISES

275

being a small book of poems by
Paul Blackburn

CAPE GOLIARD PRESS

LONDON 1968

Credits: some of these poems have appeared in: *Art Voices; Choice; Fuck You: A Magazine of the Arts; Helicon; Magazine* (ed. Ellingham & Franks); *Matter; Pogamoggan; TISH* (Vancouver); and the *Yale Literary Magazine. The Watchers* is printed by permission of *The New Yorker* © 1966.

N.B. No 206.61459.4 Cloth
"   206.61460.8 Paper
Lib OF CONGRESS No. 68-23535

The Ale House Poems

To Harry, Dorothy, & Danny, without whom, etc.; then to John, Tony, Adam, Joe Spuds, Danny Lynch, Richard, Brian, Matty, and George who facilitate the flow, or have done so; and not least to Bob Reardon, Bill Fitzgibbon, Scotty, Bob Bowles and at least 3 other Bobs, Tony, Terry, Tom, Kurt, David, 2 Georges, Wilbur, Gil, Dan Rice, and to their respective wives and girlfriends for their patience in waiting at home or outside the door. And in memory, to Jim Johnson and LeRoi Jones.

DIRECTIONS TO GET THERE

I go wherever my feet will carry me
       Sometimes the compass
             swings
                     one way,
            sometimes an-
other

Which way is the wind blowing today?
                   and
How did that compass get in there?

THE FEET!

NIGHT CAPPY

O, Danny Lynch be sittin below there in McSorley's
having an India Pale & a porter & a bit o' conversation & I
not joinin him, what whith his black eye an' all.

> Instead,
> I come direct up to bed,
> wheer the wife do be readin the newspaper
> & don't even move over for me.

I understand what the solution is, but
what be the question ?

He t'ought it were a weddin but
it was a funeral . So ?

> what is the question . or,
> who is a friend of the groom ?

THE METAMORPHOSIS

THE LADY, reclining, de-
clines, and
no mended head know what
       be her inclinations
       Still, eyes look out
       it are the rites—

And the map of Ireland
("Ireland free
from the center to the sea"
       it wails)
with the Northern Counties torn off by a passionate hand
is taped to the cupboard wall in that same public room

       The glasses' bottoms thunk down hard
         this late hour before closing,
         and some indignant horse, an
         aroused horse,
     clambers to its feet

   about to become an automobile

MOTHER, IN THE 45¢ BOTTLE

SLOW LINES lay down the curve, curve
from Astor Place & Cooper Square down,
center in the eye into
Third
Avenue, the
Bowery, the parallel lines
of light the cock lies limp inside of lines
that join at the top and bottom some old prick
lying curled drunk in the doorway
                              (the parallel
lines of sleep under the blue argon lights on his old face
down, join at the top and bottom, Cooper Square into Bowery
                              (parallel lines of

For better or worse,
lights, bars of light
in sickness & in periodic
imitation of death, the fierce
lust in sleep
stiffening of old men

RITUAL X. : The Evening Pair of Ales

EAST OF EDEN
is mountains & desert
until you cross the passes into India   .
It is 3 o'clock in the afternoon or
twenty of 8 at night, depending
             which clock you believe .

AND WEST IS WEST
It's where the cups and saucers are,
the plates, the knives and forks .

             The turkey sandwich comes alone
                or with onions if you like
The old newspaperman always takes his hat off
& lays it atop the cigarette machine;
the younger, so-hip journalist, leaves his on
old-style .

The old man sits down in the corner, puts
             his hat back on.   No challenge, but
                it's visible, the beau geste .
                   The cigarette
hangs from the side of the younger man's mouth, he's
putting himself on .
             East of Eden is mountains & desert & every
                thing creeps up on you & comes in the night,
                   unexpectedly .
when one would least put out his hand
to offer, or to defend .

MOTIVATIONS I.

each animal
his own gravedigger

    —L.Z.

Crow. Crow. Where
    leave you
my other boys?

    —L.J.

He gets a job as a waiter because

he wd/ like to look at a chef's hat
what he misses in the street

the street

THE ASSASSINATION OF PRESIDENT McKINLEY

                    Before Trinity Church
                    on lower Broadway
            3:30–3:35 P.M.
while the casket was being lowered into
the grave at Canton, Ohio,

the portals of giant buildings draped in black,
flags flying at half-mast,
the street is jammed dead with people,
maybe half of the men in bowlers and caps
the other half with their heads bared . Some

twenty Lex & Columbus Ave. & Broadway trolleys
stopped as far back as the eye can see on a muggy day,
most everyone jamming the windows murmuring or silent
while the bells of Trinity tolled for 5 minutes .

                    At Jackson Bros., at 66,
            the first-floor windows equally draped, the drapers,

black, one of the brothers takes
advantage in the back of the store
of the dead stop, of
the new little typist in accounting, makes
her bend over the great rolls of fabric
in the stockroom, lifts the voluminous skirt, pulls
down the sad white bloomers,
            undoes his fly,

　　　　　　spits on the end of his cock, &

　　　　　　　　　　fucks her, the last rite

for the assassinated Mr. McKinley,

　　　　　　　　　　September 19, 1901

Five minutes of hushed silence, the
bells booming and
schluk-schluk, the soppy petals of cunt, the groans, &
Tyley Jackson's yell of come is drowned, gone
under the final two strokes of Trinity's bell .

GETTING A JOB

How can we stand the soup?
How can we love the pope?
How can we put up with the cops?
                        and we do . . .

But plenty
of Dante
destroys us,
that great light over us

And the light enters the asshole
and the asshole enters the office
and the office records it .

THE ACTION

The old man eats
potato chips
from a brown bag

he has brought al–
most surreptitiously
into McSorley's, which

he eats with a blank stare as
he sips at his pair of ales

his hat perfect–
ly level across his temple

concealing most of his white hair
His eyes are blue

and water hard .

WIND FROM THE SOUTH AT 12 m.p.h.

High tail
wagging in the breeze

salope   that slope and
sleepy-breasted walk

as the girl in the lee
vies .

OBIT PAGE

O god.
First the greatest right-handed batter in history
Rogers Hornsby
                        (hit . 424 in 1924)
             with a lifetime average of .358

and now William Carlos Williams

                              Jan 5
                              Mar 4
                              1963

AT&T HAS MY DIME

After your voice's frozen anger
emptied the air between us, the
silence of electrical connections
the vacant window pale, the
connection broken : :

                    breaks in now
empty bravado of bar conversation, some
lonesome truck shifting gears

uptown on the avenue . Winter

has come much closer
Buy myself an ale
Manage to get it down
somehow .

TWO SONGS FOR THE OPP

1.   Stay drunk!
                that's my motto .
                Then you'll never have to know
                if the girl love you or no
                                (hee hee hee
                                now will she

2.   Play gui–
                tar, go to the bar
                hope there's one hand will caress
                and undress
                But pints to go
                before you sleep
                                (har, har,
                                nobody care

ON THE ROCKS

Small,
Polish they told him, bar, East 7th Street
Saturday nights
is the only one still open after 2 A. M.
            hence
                        crowded . to so prowl .

Even crowded is cool and quiet:
the bowling machine in one corner keeps the score
            with little clicks, sighs, and bells, the
jukebox down the wall turned down from concert size
                        no blare . the bar
packed, tables in the back near–empty .

        JUKEBOX : Slav, Slovene, Russian, Polish, Hun-
        garian, all that lonely, impassioned
        schwarze sigeuner, the violin catguts
        to tear the heart if it be torn already.

        Whose is not?

Midsummer madness by the sea at night, *las
olas doblandose siempre*
                        knees dug into the cool sand
                        Couples spread out between the
rocks hiding from the beams of
policecars patrolling boardwalk

He arranges the blanket properly
          properly
waves slosh among the rocks

One feels an intruder and walks
          away
          slowly
          back
toward the lights, the light surf repe-
titious,   dull in the ear .

                    The lovers will swim forever.
                    The whole night.

          Coming out of the bar, slosh, the waves, lovers
          sleep lightly, their hot life away for a while, their
          arms, coming out of the bar violins, gulls sleep
                    on the waves
                    cry at his back
          until the door closes . streets wet
                                        the summer rain

Reflections more shimmering and real than
the lights, dull surf, than any wall
where the mind goes blank .

THE ISLAND

Six men stand at the bar
Seven men sit at the tables
                now eight
                        now nine
a sixteenth man in the urinals
Matty behind the bar
George in the back .
Silence there is & 2 conversations
                    sometimes 3 .
It is March 9th, 3:30 in the afternoon

The loudest sound in this public room
is the exhaust fan in the east window
            or the cat at my back
                asleep there in the sun
                        bleached tabletop, golden
                            shimmer of ale .

IN WINTER

All evidence
of birds is queer,   the

square (it is not
square, inter-
section of 9th & 10th Streets, Second Avenue, near

     (& within the grounds)
   of a church called St. Mark's in-the-Bouwerie
(it is off the Bowery
at least a block of the Bowery) Bouwerie = -ing farmland
& in this case, the Pieter Stuyvesant farm, well, this square

     is
     filled
     with . young . trees
     which in this case on

a minus-20 morning in February, are filled
        with sparrows
       screaming
as tho this snow were a spring rain somehow

   Another day (same month) another
   occurrence is clearer : off the Battery
   against an ice-blue sky, some gulls
so soundlessly, the
sound of their wings is all, they
     glide above the backs of boats, stern,
     up, crying, or surrealisticly quiet .

And .
in the body and wings of each bird . are . go —

SUMMER CLOUDS / HIGH AND

SWIFT AGAINST THE HORIZON

                                        or else the snow .

THE SLOGAN

Over the right
triangle formed
by Stuyvesant St. & Ninth, the
wellknit blonde in a blue knit dress & the hair piled high

crosses on the hypotenuse, jiggles

t
w
o

w
o
r
l
d
s

& several hemispheres as she walks .

                      The trajectory

causes a mass cessation of work
at a Con Edison encampment on
one of the other two sides, all
orange equipment with dark red flashers, flags
at the corners of the encampment wave cheerfully
in the Monday morning breeze, all the orange helmets
facing the same way, eyes right, and clearly

everything else is right

Click
click

the heels go at an easy pace across Stuyvesant
touch the curb at Ninth, jiggle-jiggle . The
                explanation
is printed on the sides of all the equipment, even on one flag :
      DIG WE MUST

They dig .

POOR DOG

Out of the back window
from the wash hung two storeys up
water drops fall in the sun

slant past my floor on the light breeze
The filthy trees in my mind are never chopped down
are hung with bells tinkle in the light wind

in the light . From sunlight,
lowering the bucket into the deep well
hauled up again, tackle creaking, filled

with clear, cold
some water always slops from the zinc rim back
down, hear

waterdrops fall thru the blackness, scream,
splat, slop from the bucket, fuck it,
lift in both hands and drink

guzzling, holding the asses of young girls in our hands
drinking it all in, coffee or cream or both,
both sweet remembrance of

making it . not a thing on our minds
The silly-assed hard-drinking nights of our youth
and just making it to the bathroom in time

with shits the next morning,
warm shit leaking from our cracks .
15 years later we still talk . all night . The day

the black cat sits in the front window looking
out of our minds
down into the street with glazed eyes

screaming
at intervals
about her cunt-hole by Geoffrey,

letting the males know where she is
wanting to be where the boys are
or at least down in front of McSorley's

huddled, accepting their courtship,
watching the flies buzz
and the dog trot sidling past on a leash

interested,
not a thought on his mind,
but that eager innocent curiosity leaking

out of his muzzle, his ears, his musculature as he moves
past the cats
preparing to copulate

not a thought on their minds, sheer
intention, passive, passion, action
CAMERA, yellow filter for bright sunlight, their eyes

glaze .
They ignore him

OLD QUESTION

(*for Fee*)

Why has life put such
a need to talk inside us,
when there is nobody to talk to?

The Bakery Poems

THE BAKERY POEMS

To Mrs., Angela, Mary, Milly, and all the rest; and to Funk & Wagnalls, Drenka Willen, and the New International Year Book for being in 24th St. all those years.

A DULL POEM

(for L.Z.)

—ZEN FOODS
it says on the truck outside,
what can be
seen thru the bakery door
Third Avenue & 24th
where it is lunchtime
Saturday . The truck has blocked :
a young man with a portfolio from
the art school next block, he
walks very straight, proud, walked,
disappeared behind truck where
he can see, I can't,

        two boys making a fire
        in a can in a
        vacant lot across the avenue.
        Extends the depth of one building but
        was an half-block of tenements
        a year agone, half the way to
        25th . The wood was wet, was set
        before the truck came in and parked,
        and smoked . No cherries here, no
        mickies there. It's wet, I wonder
        what there might be in that truck
        —ZEN FOODS
        bean sprouts and rice, all of
        Chinatown's fowl & fish & vegetable,
        Zen Foods, no mickies.

Does this generation know
about mickies, set among coals, wood
fires in vacant lots, cooked to half–
raw & eaten with stolen salt / charred skins and all?
Even in those islands of still–poor Irish, their
isolated blocks about the city? No micks here
no cherries there, bean sprouts with rice &
comidas criollas composed of the obscure parts of dead pigs.
The bakery's German & serves
healthy, bland, Mitteleuropa
meals for about a buck. Tender

                        loin tomorrow,

                        goulash today.

I bring my own wine.

—ZEN FOODS—

                        Two elderly men
with long overcoats from third–hand shops
look at me meanly, leaving, wishing
the wine were theirs, mutter. The boys
in the lot appear throwing rocks,
broken Ignatz brick, at one another & jeering, no
micks here, no krauts there, no

Some seven–year–olds outside the plate glass
window are trying to liberate

                        my bicycle, it
is too securely locked to a leg
of a NO PARKING sign, garnished with

           METERED PARKING and the meters as well.

They try the lamp and go see if
some eight-year-old friend has been gifted with
a screwdriver.

    The waitress starts again
to come on, always a bit crude. That ends.
I am returned to the hopeless scene, having
     the dollar to pay. I pay,
leave tip, the
    —ZEN FOOD truck pulls out.
      "How many crullers?"
      "Two."

I do too.

THE DESPAIR

THE *a* of the Ballantine truck reversed is

/ 6

less than 7,
twice 3, that
a/6 reversed again

reflects upon

the face of a small man in a grey hat
reading the menu in the bakery window .

Features recede behind two layers of glass,

corner of the window

a/6 sits

where his face should be — is

turns it

to a skull, the man is helpless, it
is his skullface looks in
at my shadow (right) not at me
THE NUMBER 6 is the number of
fecundity in Mediterranean myth .

3 . 7 . 6 . = sixteen
a proper age, it is
my own virginity I take
The skull my own, both bodies, hers, given
ashara
it is the number 10 . color is black
A SKULL
t h e   m a n   i s   h e l p l e s s   b e f o r e   i t

SCOFFING IT

The blind man with the Wallace Beery
whiskey voice keeps bawling
"Mary!
Angie!"
tells Aunt Ella:
        "*Feel* that bread!
         I gave pigs
         better bread,
         when I had pigs
         Pennsylvania 1918."

        "When?" says Aunt Ella.

        "1918!" and he
             knocks over his glass of Pepsi.

SUNFLOWER ROCK

             "C'mon, get out,

               y'gotta get out," sez Milly,

                "stop sleeping'n get out, I call the cop."

The old man

crumples up his check and drops it onto the sawdust floor.

"Mary," he says, and staggers to his feet and

begins to come on to Mary behind the counter. She

wipes the glass counter and does not meet his eyes,

says, "You'll get out now."

He does, stiffening his body and pushing it back

off the counter with his arms, reels

              lightly toward the door:

                  "See ya tomorrow, Mary," and

                        something else low.

                            "You'll get out," she says.

                                He does.

Milly the waitress is full of plump wrath and righteousness

finding the unpaid, crumpled bill on the floor: "He

comes in, eats, he goes ta sleep,

don't even pay his bill!" Milly

lays the crumpled paper on the counter.

             I suppose there's a place to put it.

"Hey, he's all right, he

just thinks it's a flophouse!" Aunt

Ella joins in, having emerged from the kitchen

where she is these nights,
    wipes her hands on her apron
        and grins .

        "Sunstroke!" it's Max,
            a customer at the front table,
            "He wuz
            hit in that head widda sunflower!"
            makes the finger-gesture
            to his own head.
He sports a new pair of those half-sized aluminium crutches
crippled open on the chair beside him.

The circles grow from the stone.
Woodie, black dog with a curly tail,
circles back of the counter, out front again.
The Mrs. circles up from the ovens to find out
what the shouting's about . Mary
circles back of the register for someone who does pay .
Aunt Ella circles back to the kitchen,
another order's in .

Struck in the head with a sunflower,
the old man's circle has taken him out the door
            into the rain.
        Outside,
                the night is full of March rain,
                    That was the joke,
some joke . and the evening traffic uptown .

Soon,
we step into it ourself, stop
to buy a half-pint at the corner
for the cold night, for the pocket.
Already wet, we turn our back to the northwind,
feel the whiskey burn .

THIS IS NOT THE SAME AS SHARING
ANYONE ELSE'S DESPAIR

BRIGHT SUNLIGHT
on the avenue
Green & cream
        the buses,
red & cream, the buses   .
black . beige . red & cream
black . beige . red & cream
          the cars
             uptown.

Black dog in a red harness
        looks in at the door .
Old man
out of harness, looks
       in, at the door .
          "I haven't seen one of 'em yet .
          I haven't seen one like'm yet,"
says Aunt Ella looking out the door

             "My old man."
You can tell by the tone she means her
       husband.
      "Since he died,"
          she continues,
   "I HAVEN'T MET ANYONE ELSE/"

Aunt Ella's cross is people, don't
know the names of things .

"Is that carroway seed?" asks a lady
in a fur coat better than most. "No,
                    them's poppyseeds," says Aunt
Ella, & to the first conversation, confirming, "that's
why I never married again . Fifteen,
twenny dollas a night he usta spend."

                    Very loud.

Old woman with kerchief round her head &
had come in holding one hand over the heart,
                    the man's tweed jacket, the
                    heart she is wearing, sends
                    the barley soup back

"It is
too salty," she says.
The cook sends back a cream of potato
soup.
Over which she is silent, but makes eating noises .
Her face is half-eaten away .

Aunt Ella still on the register :
the guy two tables away hits the Saturday-waitress for
ten . He's her boyfriend
                    and's eating free . He
                    wears a cream nylon tie
with blue & red stripes & a midnite-blue jacket .

The tie is terrible
She loves him . Aunt
                  Ella to her interlocutor in
                  an old army overcoat & grey hair,
                  from no context
shouts reflectively,
                  "Someday!"

Bright sunlight on the avenue
Green & cream, the buses,
red & cream, the buses .
           black . beige . red & cream
           black . beige . red & cream
the cars
uptown .

THE CRISIS : a few notes

"There's two of us going,
d'ja hear, Aunt Ella?
Do they still pay ya for carrying out the bodies?"

(Bellevue Hospital)

You name it. You
    kin have it.
       Let me
           remember
the late, let us call it, crisis.

I, anyway, had a tendency to
               turn into an
inaccurate, walking, and revised Bartlett.

"Wellya know an' doncha kennit an'
haven't I told ya, every tellin' has a
talin' and that's the he an'the she of it"
           That's the *K* and the *K* of it
           That's the *A* by *Z* of it
           That's the vine, the
grapevine :

      Walkin' inta a bar at 3:30 in tha mornin'
      and a man buys me a drink because that's
      maybe the last nice thing he can do for anyone on earth—

                    at this point we're waiting
for the first Soviet ship to confront the blockade —

                         six hours away?
four? sixteen? it's happened already?

                                        (it had)

And to think
of the politicians, the poor
politicians, or statesmen, if you will
working the night out, the dis-
patches, the catches, the bastion, the
question:
           PRIME —

        "To be or not to be, that is the
           question: whether 'tis nobler in the mind to bear
           the slings and arrows of outrageous fortune, or
           taking nuclear arms against a sea of troubles,
           and by opposing
                          /
                         end them and ourselves —"
                      is not a question .

The man leaning on the fence outside my building
           falling into the garbage cans — clank —
           at 2 A.M. one morning, screaming

        "I DON'T WANT TO FIGHT NOBODY!"
           at his old wife down the street
           trying to ignore, I think, him,

trying not to admit
that she knew him, that
he had grey hair, that by any
accident of age, there was
nothing they could do anyway,

                         not even fight, were

there such an opportunity
          — just not know him —
                         drunk and
                         screaming at her

He asked me
as I put my garbage in,
               "WHAT DO YOU WANT!"
          It was a question .
I answered as I raise any
drink, or take any
leave of anyone these days.

          "Peace," I said.

IT MIGHT AS WELL BE SPRING

6:15
is already dark on
a winter night
               in December, remember? You
               keep coming back like a song
               in January, I sed you

jan – u – wary . sunset is five-forty-seven.

    "Ven I kom to dis country
    skirts vair *dis* high
                       (the hand)
    und vit a slit, yet, in da zide,
    up to here!"

    I can't look.
Out of the steamed-up window instead, a pickup truck is
cream-colored and dark avocado-green in the street
streaked every few minutes or so with pale yellow headlights
up town on the avenue . The pickup
truck apparently delivers instead . Out of the
deli next door, figure of a man, stalks the truck, opens
the door of the truck .

    In the window, it
being night, the inside of the bakery-restaurant is
    reflected back . The waitress
is cleaning up the dishes three tables back . Watch,
          the crotch,
near where her hand lay to indicate the height (DEPTH?)
    of the slit in the dress, the
uniform is white, tight, it's night, the man
    outside opens the truck door
and climbs into the waitress's skirt
    very naturally, and
                 just below the waist.

Neither one knows,
but it might as well be spring .

PRE-LENTEN GESTURES

Thank God one tone or
one set of decibels is
not all there is.   The
Dies Irae, the radio behind me, is,
due to the mad programmer we never know, followed
by a selection of military band music.
                  How kind. I
can't help thinking of
               Ed Dorn, his line: *Why*
can't it be like this all the time?
                  "as my friend said"
the band, the binding, the
bound from one state to the next, and sometimes
                one is not even asked.
What may be revealed, given.
                    What?
              that it be revealed.

A girl comes in with her little fur hat
and wants to buy THAT
cake that looks like a group of buns in the window.
Impulse buying.   That's what it is, a group of buns.
Her young husband stands outside in
his little fur hat, smiling, superciliously.

"Foolish little girl,"
said Rudolph Valentino, smiling
to himself on the set as he read and pocketed
the bill from his tailor.

                         "What is it called?"

            "Sugar buns," says Aunt Ella
            looking at the buns themselves
as tho she were identifying some obscure layer
of geological time for a
micro-paleontologist who might know better, that her
expression not insult the girl.

                         "35¢" says Aunt Ella.
The girl drops a dime of the change, leaving.
                              Her little
husband in the door smiles as she bends
                         to pick it up.

Boy in a nicely shaped black coat and a package of
laundry, crook of his arm, who has been
not-quite-studying the menu on the window between them
glances to his left and disappears down the avenue
as the girl emerges,
readjusts his bundle.

Aunt Ella runs the squeegee over the length of the door,
the glass steamed so . it is revealed
that the red blotch
on the opposite curb is a Jaguar (cap J)
            and the blue one behind it's a Ford.
            Robin's-egg Ford

            Onward and upward,
we used to say in the army, before
trying to pick up a cluster of teenagers, the
streets of San Antone that hot,

we were that hot . A small boy has started a fire
in the vacant lot beyond the Jaguar and Ford. Sousa
still calling the sounds from the radio at my back.

I AM BACK to an earlier question:
someone had found it strange
I should think of the concommitant physical cul–
                              mination of love,
fucking, in short, as a release, some
                    times a relief from
              the pain of loving itself.

Surcease of pain. The idea
                    is medieval at least:

"o lady, give me some relief,
cure me of that sweet sickness
I am subject to"
                    object, of course,
                         bed . what
happens to impulses from fingers that touch that
smooth skin, that they skim the breast, down the
line of ribs, beneath the indentation of waist, the
flare of hip, smoothness of thigh rounding inward
past forests of night to churn among mucous membranes,
heat rising.

              The beaky crane, the
              "one–eyed great goose"
              the tower risen out of the olive grove.
              Surcease of pain.

Love, the disease that implies
its own cure, part and end of it.
And that end begins again.

"You, who alone can cure me by your touch, Lady,"
a cry they sometimes insisted was, had been
addressed to the Virgin, implied in its end

surcease of pain, no virgin, but another hand,
and that miraculous touch his lady's fingers curled
against his own, against the small of his back, flat out.

     A mystery? No . What
       else could happen? The
world is what it is, men and women what they are.
Every organic thing, o philosophers, man,
plant or animal, containing as seed the flower,
its own destruction, its own rebirth . Yeats was right?

         "All true love must die
           Alter at the best
           Into some lesser thing.
           Prove that I lie."

Hardly,
with O'Leary in the grave, seed of that growth,
cure of that ill, and
once begun, the act fore-
tells its own, what-
ever-breaking-now, its own
        end . revealed.

                    Squeegee drawn once more
               down the door's glass,
the Jaguar gone, the Ford remains itself at last,
revealed smaller now by itself, as the houses, parks,
the football fields of our youth, than
                              it / they / then /
                                   seemed .

                    It always is,
                    always was
                    this way, Ed,
                    all the time.

It is not that it does not happen.
It does,
          and there is no help for it.
          And
there is no end to it,
until there is .

THE WATCHERS

It's going to rain
Across the avenue a crane
whose name is
        CIVETTA LINK-BELT
dips, rises and turns in a
      graceless geometry

     But grace is slowness / as
ecstacy is some kind of speed or madness /
The crane moves slowly, that
much it is graceful / The men
     watch and the leaves

Cranes make letters in the sky
    as the wedge flies
        The scholar's function is

          Mercury, thief and poet,
          invented the first 7 letters
          5 of them vowels, watching
          cranes . after got

The men watch and the rain does not come
        HC - 108B CIVETTA LINK-BELT
In the pit below a yellow cat,
      CAT - 933
            pushes the debris
and earth to load CIVETTA HC - 108B
    Cat's name is PASCO and
    there is an ORegon phone number,
moves its load toward 3 piles
Let him leave the building to us

Palamedes, son of Nauplius,
   invented 11 more
                (consonant)
Also invented the lighthouse, and
measures, the scales, the disc, and
"the art of posting sentinels"
Ruled over the Mysians,
            Cretan stock, al-
            though his father was Greek
            Took part in the Trojan trouble on the
Greek side . The scholar's function is fact . Let him
          quarry cleanly . All
          THOSE INVENTIONS CRETAN
          so that a Greek / alpha-beta-tau
          based on a Cretan, not a Phoenician
          model
          Three different piles :

earth / debris / & schist, the stud/stuff of the island
     is moved by this
     PASCO
     CAT - 933
     ORegon 6-
it does not rain . smoke, the
               alpha-beta-tau

raised from   5 vowels, 13 consonants to
               5 vowels, 15 consonants
               (Epicharmus) not
the Sicilian writer of comedies, 6 A.D., but
his ancestor /
the Aesculapius family at Cos, a couple are
mentioned in the Iliad as physicians to
the Greeks before the equipotent walls
of Troy

            No, it does not rain, smoke
            rises from the engines, the
            leaves . The men watch
            before the walls of Troy

Apollo in cithaera ceteras literas adjecit

        7 strings on that zither
        & for each string a letter
        Thence to Simonides,
native of Ceos in the service of Dionysus
which god also at home in Delphos
both gods of the solar year as were /   Aesculapius
                                   & Hercules
                                   Let's
   get all of this into one pot, 6-700 years B.C.

Simonides, well-known poet, intro-
ducted into Athens 4 more letters . the
      unnecessary double-consonants *PSI*
                       (earlier written Pi-Sigma)
     and *XI* (earlier written Kappa-Sigma)
plus (plus) two vowels : *OMEGA*, a distinction from
      the omicron Hermes conned
      from the 3 Crones, and
EPSILON, as distinct from their eta
& that's the long & the short of it .

Cranes fly in V-formation & the
Tyrrhenians, or Etruscans, were
also of Cretan stock, held
the crane in reverence / The men watch
           LINK-BELT move up its load, the
           pile to the left near 24th St., the
           permanent erection moves
           slow-ly almost sensually, al-most
                 gracefully
The scholar's function / fact . Let him quarry
cleanly / leave the building to us / Poems
nicked with a knife onto the bark of a stick (Hesiod)
     or upon tablets of clay
          Perseus cuts off the Gorgon-head
             (Medusa)
          and carries it off in a bag . But

the head's a ritual mask and a protection, we
frighten children with it
and trespassers
when we perform the rites . It is
                        no murder,
                        she has given him power of sight
p o e t r y ,
                the gorgons no pursuers
                are escort, and the mask
                                (his protection)
Hermes / Car / Mercury / Perseus / Palamedes / Thoth / or
        whatever his original name was,
winged sandals and helmet, you bet!
the swiftness of poetic thought / And the bag

THE ALPHABET'S IN THE BAG!

Almost sensually, almost
gracefully . The men watch
and know not what they watch
The cat pushes . the crane . the bud
lifts upward . above the

                        Pillars of Hercules, desti-
nation, where he is going, bringing the secret in the bag
                The tree at Gades (Cádiz)
        principal city of Tartessus, the
Aegean colony on the Guadalquivir
From there the Milesians will take it to Ireland?
The older city is on the western shore with its
                Temple of Cronus   . island,
                the island of the goddess,
                Red Island / & Cronus
god of the middle finger, the fool's finger / It is
        his father he kills not his mother, his mother
        gives him
                the secret
                        Scholar's function is
                                The men watch

Hercules' shrine set up by colonists, 1100 B.C.
400 years before the Phoenicians
coming from Tyre in painted ships
        and their oracle

                    HERCULES = PALAMEDES (?)

7 & 2
9 steps to the goddess
& everyone lives to 110 years
5 years to a lustrum
                        (Etruscan)
22   lustra = 110
                        (alpha-beta-tau
& the circumferance of the circle when
      the diameter is 7 is
22
proportion known as π
22 (plus) over 7
a neat recurrent sequence
which does not work out because it never
ends /
7 lustra is 35 years . Maturity,
or the age at which a man may be elected
President of the United States / a convention
or a Roman might be elected Consul / a convention
                    $$\frac{22}{7}$$
These numbers no longer a secret / But in Crete
                                or Spain...
Spanish, the mother's family name
still is set down last, and
still in Crete descent is matrilineal
The Greeks have accomplished nothing
      but death   beauty
                (Troy)

The men watch the cat push
keeping the piles discrete
earth / debris / & schist
the stuff of the island, the crane, the bud
lifts upward . above the

And at Cádiz, Caius Julius Hyginus,
a Spaniard and Ovid's friend,
curator of the Palantine Library,
exiled from the court of Augustus

sitting under a tree in Cádiz
over the problem, over a millenium later,
traces Greek letters in the spelt of wine at his table
watches the cranes fly over toward Africa
wedge in the sunset / set down the score :

> Mercury (or the Fates)   7
> Palamedes   11
> Epicharmus   2
> Simonides   4

Say that he used Etruscan sources,
        does that explain it?
Let them quarry cleanly
        Let them leave
Cranes winging over toward Africa
        a wedge .
Hyginus traces π on the wooden table in wine spelt

    The cat pushes, the crane, the bud
    lifts upward / above the
    rain comes finally
The watchers leave the construction site,
the men leave their machines
        At 323 Third Avenue,
        an old drunk (Hyginus)
sits in a doorway and downs a whole
pint of Sacramento Tomato Juice
                    The watchers are the gods

                    The leaves burgeon

Illustrations by Michelle Stuart: "The Crisis", "The Watch-ers", "Ritual X: The Evening Pair of Ales", "On The Rocks".

This first edition was Designed, Printed & Published by Cape Goliard Press Ltd. 10a Fairhazel Gardens London N.W.6. & consists of 3500 soft cover, 1400 case bound, of which 100 are signed & numbered by the author.

2750 copies of this edition have been bound in two editions for distribution by Grossman Publishers in the United States: 2000 soft cover 750 case bound.

Printed in Great Britain.